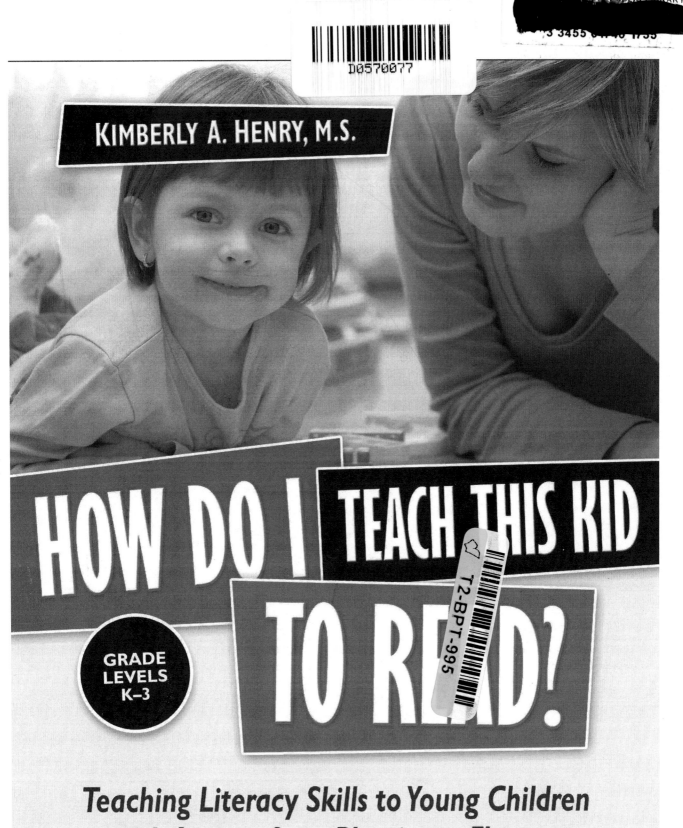

KIMBERLY A. HENRY, M.S.

HOW DO I TEACH THIS KID TO READ?

GRADE LEVELS K–3

Teaching Literacy Skills to Young Children with Autism, from Phonics to Fluency

HOW DO I TEACH THIS KID TO READ?

All marketing and publishing rights guaranteed to and reserved by

FUTURE HORIZONS INC.

721 W. Abram Street
Arlington, Texas 76013
800-489-0727
817-277-0727
817-277-2270 (fax)
Email: info@FHautism.com
www.FHautism.com

Publisher's Cataloging-In-Publication Data
(Prepared by The Donohue Group, Inc.)

Henry, Kimberly A., 1968-
  How do I teach this kid to read? : teaching literacy skills to young children with autism, from phonics to fluency / Kimberly A. Henry.

    p. : ill. ; cm. + 1 CD. -- (How do I teach this kid)

Accompanying CD contains visual materials intended to supplement the lessons.
Includes bibliographical references and index.
ISBN: 978-1-935274-14-8

  1. Autistic children--Education. 2. Reading (Early childhood) 3. Early childhood special education.
4. Autism--Popular works. I. Title.

LC4717.5 .H46 2010
371.92

TABLE OF CONTENTS

How Do I Teach This Kid to Read?
© 2010 by Kimberly A. Henry. Future Horizons, Inc.

ACKNOWLEDGEMENTS

I am a teacher, first and foremost. I am not an "expert," a researcher, or a scientist. I am an educator who enjoys sharing successful ideas and strategies with other educators. During my time working with children with autism spectrum disorders and other developmental disabilities, my most successful teaching strategies have been ones that cater to the individual needs of my students. As a firm believer in the motto "Why reinvent the wheel?", I also know that many of my strategies have been borrowed or "tweaked" from others in my profession—colleagues, workshop presenters, authors, and parents. This is what teachers do—we create, we borrow, and we refine to meet the unique needs of our students.

As such, every attempt has been made in this book to give credit to the originator of a strategy, if it is not my own. However, having been in the teaching profession for almost twenty years, it is nearly impossible to recall where or from whom some ideas originated. In these cases, it is not my intention to slight any creative person; rather, my memory has lapsed.

Thank you to all teachers, whether you teach individuals with autism or not, for your creativity, your ingenuity, and your dedication to "doing what it takes" to help each of your students grow and learn. In the spirit of sharing, I share with you my favorite ideas for building early literacy skills.

INTRODUCTION

It's simple.

"The more that you read, the more things you will know.
The more that you learn, the more places you'll go."

—Dr. Seuss

My favorite children's author said it in a rhyming, whimsical fashion in the pages of his book, *I Can Read with My Eyes Shut*. Reading takes you places—places you've been, places you'll go, and places you'll only dream about.

Reading is so much more than just letters and words on a page. Reading is communication. Reading is imagination. Reading is participation.

A love of reading can be developed early in children. Favorite stories are read over and over again, the ABC song is sung, and letters and sounds are "played with" to create rhyming and nonsense words. For many young children, reading becomes a special time to bond with a favorite adult in their lives. Reading helps them grow and vicariously experience things they are curious about, and dream about.

For young children with autism, reading is often a factual memorization of letters and words. The playful, imaginative qualities of reading may be missed in favor of the repetitive, predictable alphabet and visual appearance of words on a page.

Of course, all children with autism are different. Autism is a spectrum disorder—encompassing a wide range of strengths and challenges of children with similar learning characteristics. Each child with autism with whom I have worked has had different abilities, different needs, and different interests. However, there are several common characteristics of many children with autism that can provide the foundation for teaching them successfully. Teachers—parents and school teachers—need to understand these learning characteristics in order to develop effective instructional strategies for their students with autism.

Essentially, there are three core areas of deficit in children diagnosed with an autism spectrum disorder:

1. communication
2. socialization
3. restricted patterns of behavior and interests

Although the degree of intensity of each of these deficit areas will vary with each child, they impact his or her ability to learn and they present unique instructional challenges to teachers and families working with children who have an autism spectrum disorder.

The ability to read is an essential skill that spans a child's school-age years and beyond. Reading provides personal enjoyment, access to information, and opens doors to opportunities throughout daily life, both recreational and occupational. Because the ability to read and comprehend is closely linked to an individual's language abilities and social understanding, children with autism often struggle with the process of reading. While many children with an autism spectrum disorder, particularly those with Asperger's Syndrome or those with higher skill levels, may read fluently, comprehension is often limited because of those core deficits in communication and socialization.

Specifically, children with receptive and expressive language deficits may have difficulty understanding questions related to the text or may be unable to provide an effective answer to questions asked of them. Response to questions may be slow due to auditory processing difficulties. Because children with autism may have a restricted range of interests and limited knowledge of the world, their ability to access prior knowledge or make personal connections to text may be compromised. Socially, children with autism have difficulty relating to others, and they may not be able to appreciate the relationships, motivations, or problems of characters in a story. Children with autism are typically concrete, literal thinkers. These differences in thought processes make abstract concepts presented in text, both fiction and nonfiction, difficult for them to understand.

In the late 1990s, Congress charged the National Reading Panel (NRP), a government panel comprised of experts in the fields of reading instruction, psychology, and higher education, educational administrators, and parents, with reviewing research on reading instruction in the early grades (K-3) and identifying those techniques that led to successful reading achievement. In 2000, the panel issued a report with their findings: effective reading instruction consists of a balance of phonemic awareness, phonics, fluency, vocabulary, and text comprehension[1].

---

[1] The National Reading Panel: Teaching Children to Read—A Summary Report. (April 2000). National Institute of Child Health and Human Development.

Taking into consideration the findings of the NRP and the learning characteristics of children with autism spectrum disorders, this book presents several simple instructional strategies that can be used to help develop early literacy skills in young children with autism. The strategies are not designed to be used in isolation or exclusively. A systematic, balanced literacy program is always recommended to ensure that appropriate instruction is delivered in each area of literacy development.

All children are different. All children learn differently. A strategy that might be successful with one child may not make sense to another child. Teachers have the responsibility of finding instructional strategies that meet the needs of all of their students. Parents are a child's first teachers. As such, parents of young children often spend countless hours working with their children to introduce them to the skills they will need to be successful as they enter school and throughout life. The strategies presented in this book can be used by parents, classroom teachers, special educators, speech and language pathologists—anyone with a vested interest in developing the reading skills of a young child with autism. As always, the strategies can be adapted to meet the individual needs of children at various reading levels. Remember…

> "The more that you read, the more things you will know.
> The more that you learn, the more places you'll go."
>
> —Dr. Seuss

Have fun!

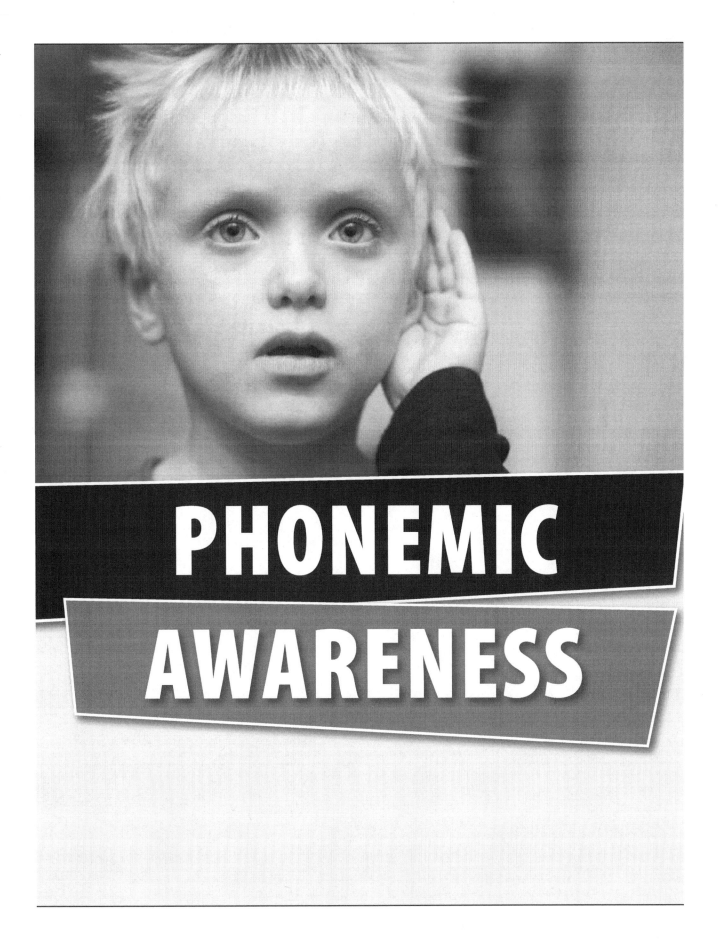

PHONEMIC

AWARENESS

PHONEMIC AWARENESS

What is phonemic awareness?

Phonemic awareness is the ability to work with individual sounds in words, called phonemes. It also incorporates the understanding that sounds work together to form words. A similar term, *phonics,* deals with the relationship between the sounds of spoken language and the letters of written language. Even though sounds and letters are two distinct components of early literacy, for the purposes of this book I will include phonics activities in the phonemic awareness section, as the techniques presented involve working with sounds, letters, and words.

Why is phonemic awareness important to reading success?

One of the most compelling and well-established findings in the research on beginning reading is the important relationship between phonemic awareness and reading acquisition.[1]

Phonemic awareness prepares readers to read print by helping them understand that letters represent sounds. When children recognize that words can be divided into sounds and sounds can be blended into words, they then have a way to decipher new words by sounding them out according to the different phonemes in the word. This is an extremely important skill, as there are far too many words in the English language to rely on sight word recognition and memorization alone (although this is often a strength of children with ASD!).

How do typically developing young children demonstrate phonemic awareness?

Young children who demonstrate beginning phonemic awareness can tell whether words are the same or different (bat/bat = same; bat/bar = different). They may play with rhyming words (sit, kit, pit, mitt, etc.). Nursery rhymes, Dr. Seuss books (my favorite!), and rhyming chants and songs all help to foster beginning phonemic awareness in young children. Explicit phonemic awareness instruction in the early years focuses on teaching children to isolate, blend, and segment sounds. Young children learn to hear the initial sound in a word (e.g., /b/ in "bat"). They know when words begin with the same letter (e.g., bat and ball). They can create the word "bat" upon hearing the sounds /b/-/a/ -/t/

---

[1] Kame'enui, E. J., Simmons, D. C., Baker, S., Chard, D. J., Dickson, S. V., Gunn, B., Smith, S. B., Sprick, M., & Lin, S. J. (1997). Effective strategies for teaching beginning reading. In E. J. Kame'enui, & D. W. Carnine (Eds.), *Effective Teaching Strategies That Accommodate Diverse Learners.* Columbus, OH: Merrill.

and they can break the word "bat" into the three component phonemes, /b/-/a/-/t/. As phonemic awareness skills develop, young children can hear the number of syllables in a word and segment multi-syllable words.

How do young children with ASD struggle with phonemic awareness?

The development of strong phonics and phonemic awareness requires adequate auditory processing skills. A child has to be able to hear and process the sounds in a word to be able to break them apart or blend them together to sound out new or unfamiliar words. Many children with autism have problems with auditory processing.

Auditory processing is not a hearing problem but a processing problem in the brain—the brain's ability to recognize and interpret sounds is affected in individuals with auditory processing disorders. This can mean that a child with auditory processing difficulties may not be able to distinguish whether the initial sound in the word "pen" is actually /p/ or /t/ or /k/. This difficulty may make the task of segmenting or blending sounds laborious and frustrating, affecting all aspects of a child's reading ability—vocabulary, fluency, comprehension, as well as the basic building-block skills of phonemic awareness.

How can phonemic awareness be developed?

Break out the Dr. Seuss and Mother Goose! Encourage playfulness with words. Read children's books and poems that highlight sounds, rhyme, and alliteration. Make a game of generating rhyming words, even nonsense words.

Have fun with mirrors! A mirror is a perfect way to play with saying and seeing sounds. Show your child how your lips and mouth look when you say a certain sound. Get your child to imitate the sound, looking in the mirror at his mouth as he vocalizes.

Even though it is a serious skill to be developed, phonemic awareness can be playful and fun and silly. Keep this sense of playfulness and fun as you work with your child to create sounds and rhymes.

How Do I Teach This Kid to Read?
© 2010 by Kimberly A. Henry. Future Horizons, Inc.

ABC BOOK
ACTIVITY

What It Is

The ABC Book is an easy-to-make, easy-to-use book that can be shared with young children to teach letters and their corresponding sounds. Both upper- and lowercase letters are presented along with the sound made by the letter. Two words that begin with each letter are also introduced.

Why It Works!

The ABC Book presents letters and sounds in both visual and auditory modes. Children are often drawn to the "sing-songy," repetitive pattern of the words and sounds. A word of caution, however: be sure to change the words associated with each letter periodically so that children do not become rigidly focused only on the two words presented initially. This book can be used with the next suggested strategy, the ABC Thematic Book, by using the same letter pages and changing the pictures to incorporate words from a theme you may be studying.

Materials Needed

- ❏ ABC Book Letter Pages from the CD
- ❏ ABC Book Picture Pages from the CD
- ❏ Velcro® dots
- ❏ 3" or 4" binder for containing the pages

Directions for Assembly

1. From the CD, print the ABC Book Letter Pages. (Both portrait and landscape pages are provided. The photo to the right shows the landscape option.)
2. Then print the ABC Book Picture Pages.
3. Laminate the letter pages and picture pages.
4. Place two pieces of soft loop Velcro above the letters on the letter pages.

The Picture Communication Symbols ©1981–2010 by Mayer-Johnson LLC. All Rights Reserved Worldwide. Used with permission. Boardmaker™ is a trademark of Mayer-Johnson LLC.

5. Cut out the pictures and place hook Velcro on the back of each picture.

6. Match the pictures to the correct letter pages.

7. Punch holes in the pages and insert into a 3" or 4" binder.

Ideas for Use

- Read each page in a sing-song fashion: "Apple, alligator, a, a, a" (short "a" sound). Student can repeat after you.

- Read each page in the manner described above, omitting the third letter sound and have students say the sound to complete the page (e.g., "Apple, alligator, a, a, ____").

- Read/sing only the pictures and have the students read/sing the letter sounds.

- Remove one picture from each page and have students locate the correct picture to complete the page from a field of distracters. Then proceed to "read" each page in the previously mentioned fashion.

- Remove both pictures from the pages and have students place the correct pictures on each page. Then proceed to "read" each page.

Original source unknown. I first borrowed this idea from the Sorensen family—thank you!

PRINTABLE TOOLS ON THE CD

ABC Book Letter Pages
Portrait & Landscape

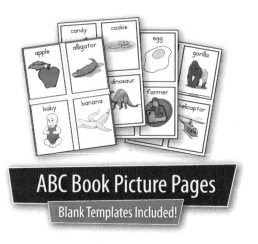

ABC Book Picture Pages
Blank Templates Included!

THEMATIC ABC BOOK

ACTIVITY

What It Is

The Thematic ABC Book is a variation on the ABC Book strategy. Words related to the thematic unit being studied are paired with each letter of the alphabet. BONUS: This strategy not only helps to build phonemic awareness skills, but is a vocabulary builder as well!

Why It Works!

The Thematic ABC Book presents letters and sounds in both visual and auditory modes. The book created in the previous strategy, the ABC Book, can be used with this variation. Simply use the same alphabet pages, but change the words to reflect thematic vocabulary.

Materials Needed

- ❏ ABC Book Letter Pages from the CD
- ❏ Thematic pictures to represent two words for each letter
- ❏ Velcro® dots
- ❏ 3" or 4" binder for containing the pages

Directions for Assembly

1. From the CD, print each letter page.
2. Print each page of pictures.
3. Laminate the letter pages and pictures.
4. Place two pieces of soft loop Velcro above the letters on the letter pages.
5. Cut out the pictures and place hook Velcro on the back of each picture.
6. Match the pictures to the correct letter pages.
7. Punch holes in the pages and insert into a 3" or 4" binder.

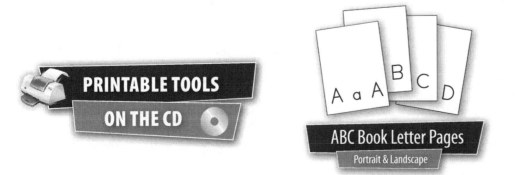

PRINTABLE TOOLS ON THE CD

ABC Book Letter Pages
Portrait & Landscape

ABC ACTION CHANT
ACTIVITY

What It Is

The ABC Action Chant is a chant that can be used with young children to teach letters and their corresponding sounds. A word that is associated with each letter and sound is also introduced.

Why It Works!

The ABC Action Chant is a multi-sensory learning strategy! The auditory chant has an established rhythm and pattern that young children will tune in to. Picture cue cards can be used along with the auditory chant to visually represent the letters and the associated word. The actions associated with each letter, sound, and word provide kinesthetic input for those students who learn best through movement. Plus, the chant is a lot of fun!

Materials Needed

❏   Cue cards and/or chart made from ABC Action Chant Pictures

Directions for Assembly

1.   From the CD, print the ABC Action Chant Pictures.
2.   Cut each picture out, mount on sturdy card stock, and laminate if desired.

A Handy Tip

The ABC Action Chant Pictures can be glued onto poster board and made into a large chart, with all the letters visible at one time, if you prefer.

Thank you Laura Christy, Kindergarten teacher, for sharing the idea with me and allowing me to adapt it for my students!

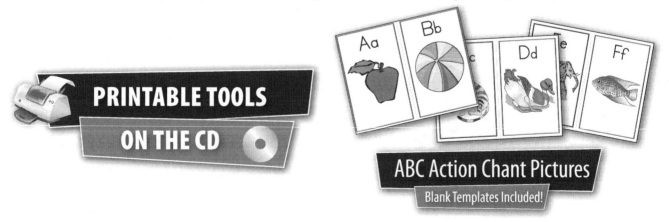

PRINTABLE TOOLS
ON THE CD

ABC Action Chant Pictures
Blank Templates Included!

ABC Action Chant

LETTER	WORD	ASSOCIATED ACTION
A	apple	Pretend you are picking an apple off a tree and taking a bite.
B	ball	Pretend you are bouncing a ball.
C	cat	Make cat whiskers using both hands.
D	duck	Make a duck beak with two fingers and thumb by your mouth.
E	elephant	Place one hand at your nose and curve it down like an elephant trunk.
F	fish	Pretend your hand is a fish and "swim."
G	giggle	Pretend you are laughing.
H	hi	Wave as if you are saying "hi" to someone.
I	inch	With fingers and thumb, measure one inch.
J	jump	Jump out of the chair.
K	kite	Pretend you are flying a kite.
L	lap	Put hands in lap.
M	mix	Pretend you are mixing in a bowl.
N	no	Shake your head "no."
O	octopus	Lock your thumbs and let your eight fingers wiggle around like an octopus.
P	pig	Make a pig nose—push up your nose.
Q	quiet	Bring your index finger up to your mouth (do NOT say "sh").
R	rabbit	Take two hands and make them rabbit ears.
S	snake	Wiggle your index finger like a snake.
T	turtle	Place one hand over the other and stick out the thumb on the bottom hand (as if a turtle's head).
U	umbrella	Pretend to put up an umbrella.
V	violin	Pretend you are playing a violin.
W	wiggle	Wiggle around in your seat.
X	x-ray	Move your arm up and down the front of your body as if you are scanning it.
Y	yo-yo	Pretend you are playing with a yo-yo.
Z	zipper	Pretend you are pulling up a zipper.

What It Is

Fridge Phonics® is a magnetic letter set produced by LeapFrog Enterprises, Inc. It contains 26 magnetic letters and a "magic reader" that recognizes each letter as it is placed inside and tells the letter name and sound made by the letter. An additional feature, the music note button, sings the alphabet song when pressed. The letter reader and individual letters can attach to any magnetic surface for ease of use.

Why It Works!

Fridge Phonics is fun! It is a hands-on tool for learning letters and corresponding letter sounds. It provides a kinesthetic, visual, and auditory way for young children to learn letters and letter sounds.

Materials Needed

❑ Fridge Phonics® can be purchased from LeapFrog Enterprises, Inc., online at www.leapfrog.com or in many local stores that sell toys.

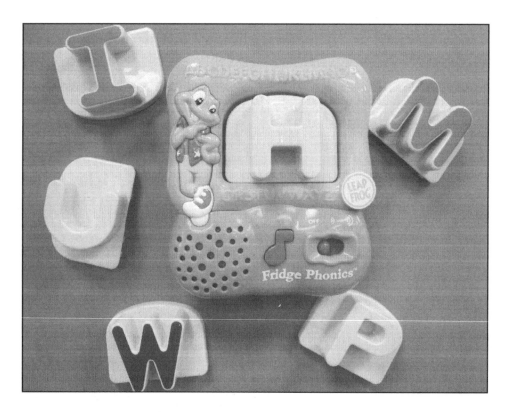

DR. SEUSS & FRIENDS
ACTIVITY

What It Is

Many favorite children's stories are full of rhymes, alliteration, and lively play with the sounds of language. Dr. Seuss, one of my favorite children's authors, is the master of such word play! His books include rhyming, repetition, and creative characters, making them a favorite with both adults and children. Dr. Seuss often uses silly or nonsensical words to create a rhyme—that's okay! The crazy sounds of the words and the antics of his outrageous characters make children want to hear the books read aloud over and over again!

Why It Works!

Dr. Seuss carefully crafted his books to develop language, phonemic awareness, and beginning reading skills. And as an added bonus—they are lots of fun! Many children with ASD are attracted to the repetitive rhythms and rhymes of Dr. Seuss stories. Parents and teachers can encourage an early love of language and word-play by making Dr. Seuss books and others like them (see book list) a regular part of a child's routine. However, if the child you are working with is bothered by nonsensical words, objects, and/or creatures, you may want to stick with more true-to-life stories and books.

Materials Needed

❑ A fun collection of books! (The included booklist may get you started and is not all-inclusive by any means! Your local librarian can recommend other age-appropriate books that help develop phonemic awareness.)

Ideas for Reading

1. Read aloud in an animated fashion. Show your child how much fun language can be!

2. Phonemic awareness begins with sounds. When reading a book such as Dr. Seuss's *Mr. Brown Can Moo, Can You?* (my personal favorite, by the way!), see if your child can imitate each of the sounds after you. Have fun with the sounds—say them softly, loudly, slowly, quickly—the possibilities are limited only by your imagination!

3. Once your child is familiar with a text and has heard it many times, pause at the end of a rhyming line to see if your child can supply the word that completes the rhyme.

4. For books that use rhyming nonsense words, see if your child can create a nonsense word that rhymes, too, using a different initial letter. For example, if an author writes about a character called "zat" (that looks like a cat—and rhymes, too!), see if your child can create a different name for the character that also rhymes with "cat" and "zat."

5. When reading a book like Dr. Seuss's ABC Book that generates many words beginning with a certain letter, see how many more words your child can think of that begin with that same letter.

Suggested Books for Developing Phonemic Awareness

A, My Name Is Alice
    by Jane E. Bayer

Barnyard Banter
    by Denise Fleming

Chugga-Chugga Choo-Choo
    by Kevin Lewis

Clickety Clack
    by Rob Spence and Amy Spence

Down By the Bay
    by Raffi

Dr. Seuss's ABC
    by Dr. Seuss

Each Peach Pear Plum
    by Allan Ahlberg and Janet Ahlberg

*Eating the Alphabet:
Fruits & Vegetables from A to Z*
    by Lois Ehlert

Fox in Socks
    by Dr. Seuss

Frozen Noses
    by Jan Carr

Green Eggs and Ham
    by Dr. Seuss

Hop on Pop
    by Dr. Seuss

"I Can't" Said the Ant
    by Polly Cameron

I Know an Old Lady Who Swallowed a Fly
    by Colin Hawkins and Jacqui Hawkins

I Love You, Good Night
    by Jon Buller and Susan Schade

Jake Baked the Cake
    by B. G. Hennessy

The Listening Walk
    by Paul Showers

The Little Old Lady Who Was Not Afraid of Anything
    by Linda Williams

Millions of Snowflakes
    by Mary McKenna Siddals

Miss Spider's ABC
  by David Kirk

Moses Supposes His Toeses Are Roses
  by Nancy Patz

Mr. Brown Can Moo, Can You?
  by Dr. Seuss

Mrs. Wishy Washy
  by Joy Cowley

On Market Street
  by Arnold Lobel

Sheep in a Jeep
  by Nancy Shaw

Stop That Noise!
  by Paul Geraghty

There's a Wocket in My Pocket!
  by Dr. Seuss

Tumble Bumble
  by Felicia Bond

The Z Was Zapped
  by Chris Van Allsburg

MAGIC WORD BOOK
ACTIVITY

What It Is

A Magic Word Book is an interactive, visual tool for learning "word family" words. The book is comprised of a back page and a series of flip cards layered on top. The back page contains targeted rimes—the vowel and the letters following it (e.g., –at as in hat); the flip cards contain the onset—the letter or letters that come before the vowel in the word (e.g., h– as in hat)

Why It Works!

Magic Word Books are visual and predictable. Magic Word Books can be customized to address different learning needs or difficulty levels. You may even find uses for them other than the "word family" application described here! But be aware that word families may confuse lower-functioning children, as it may be difficult for them to blend the two parts visually and/or auditorily. Use your best judgement.

Materials Needed

- ❏ Card stock or other heavy paper for back page
- ❏ Another piece of card stock, cut in half vertically, or cut into individual flip cards
- ❏ A method of binding the "book"—spiral binding, individual binder rings, a three-ring binder, etc.—anything that works for you!

Directions for Assembly

You can create this book by using the A, E, I O, U, and blank word pages on the CD. Or, you can make the pages by hand with markers:

1. Divide the back page into two columns with four equal size boxes in each.
2. Write the rimes (e.g., –at) to be used in the right hand column, as close to the left margin as possible.
3. The left hand column of the back page can remain blank or can be programmed with four onsets (e.g., h– as in hat) that match the rimes in the corresponding spots in the right column.

4. Write four onsets that match the rimes in the left column on the half-sheet of card stock or individual flip cards. Write the onsets as close to the right margin as possible. Include an illustration if needed to provide a visual prompt for the complete word. Make as many "right hand columns/flip cards" as you care to program.

5. Bind the "book" on the left side in a three-ring binder, with spiral binding, or with individual binder rings.

The Picture Communication Symbols ©1981–2010 by Mayer-Johnson LLC. All Rights Reserved Worldwide.
Used with permission. Boardmaker™ is a trademark of Mayer-Johnson LLC.

DIPHTHONG SONG

ACTIVITY

What It Is

The Diphthong Song is a song I created to help my students remember the sounds associated with letter combinations. It's just a fun little song—you can create your own songs for other letter combinations or for different purposes, using familiar tunes and pictures for visual cues. (The song actually contains digraphs and diphthongs—I just call it a "diphthong song" because it rhymes!)

Why It Works!

The Diphthong Song uses music to teach the concept of letter combinations and sounds. Many of my students are interested in music, and I have found it to be a powerful learning tool for teaching students some relatively difficult concepts. The tendency of students who have learned the sound for each letter of the alphabet is to say each letter sound (s-h-i-r-t). Presenting the letter combinations as one sound in a song helps them see the sound as a whole rather than separate sounds.

Materials Needed

❑ A printout of the Diphthong Song from the CD

Sample verse: (to the tune of "Jingle Bells")

S-H, S-H, S-H says /sh/

Shirt and ship and sheep and shoes

S-H says /sh/

Diphthong Song

VOCABULARY

VOCABULARY

What is vocabulary?

Vocabulary is the ability to understand and use words to acquire and convey information. Vocabulary can be broken into two different areas: expressive vocabulary and receptive vocabulary. Expressive vocabulary is the ability to speak or write a specific word for a specific meaning. Receptive vocabulary is the ability to associate a specific meaning with a word encountered in reading or listening.

Why is vocabulary important to reading success?

The size of a child's vocabulary has a direct correlation with his or her reading comprehension and reading fluency. The size of a child's vocabulary affects his comprehension abilities: if he doesn't know what a word means, he will have difficulty understanding its meaning in context. Also, without a large vocabulary, children stumble on words as they read, are puzzled by the meaning of words, and their reading becomes choppy and confusing.

How do typically developing young children demonstrate vocabulary?

Typically developing two-year-olds and three-year-olds often bombard others with the question, "What's that?" This innate (and sometimes incessant!) questioning is their way of learning the names of objects in their environment. They often "try out" their new words by using them in conversation and creating longer sentences with them as they speak.

How do young children with ASD struggle with vocabulary?

Actually, vocabulary is often a relative strength for children with autism spectrum disorders. Young children may be very good at naming objects in their environment because much of their language instruction focuses on building vocabulary and answering "what" questions.

However, being able to transfer the idea of a concrete object to a word encountered in text sometimes presents a challenge. Encountering a word in text is more abstract than seeing an object "in the flesh" and naming it.

Children with ASD often have difficulty transferring knowledge to a new situation or referent after learning it. For example, one of my former students had a dog. His dog was a Labrador, a relatively big dog. When we read a story that contained a Poodle, he had difficulty understanding that this smaller, "fancier" dog was actually a dog, too. His understanding of the word "dog" was linked to his big, black Lab—a very different-looking dog than the little, white Poodle in the story.

How can vocabulary be developed?

Talk to your child. Talk about many different topics. Name objects, people, and events in your daily routine. Use synonyms for words to expand your child's vocabulary beyond the known and familiar. Conversations with young children are a fun and easy way to introduce new words.

Draw your child's attention to the printed word in everyday settings. Point out words on store logos, food containers, traffic signs, building signs, and items around the house. Focus your child's attention to vocabulary in books by pointing to words and pictures as you read.

Provide experiences for your child to learn new vocabulary concretely before encountering it in a text. For example, if a character in a story is eating a food that is unfamiliar to your child, try to obtain that food and—ideally—have your child taste it (but, for many reasons, this may not be possible!), or at least allow your child to look at the new food, touch it, and smell it. Write down the name of the food so your child sees it. Then, as your child encounters the word in the text, he has some prior experience and may be able to make an easier connection between this new vocabulary word and the actual food item he encountered earlier. This hands-on learning also builds your child's repertoire of experiences, which helps to enhance reading comprehension skills as well!

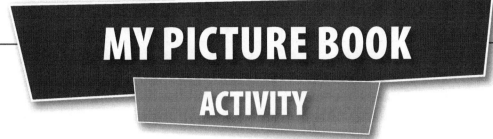

MY PICTURE BOOK
ACTIVITY

What It Is

My Picture Book is a strategy for early vocabulary building. Each book is individualized using pictures or photos of items that are of special interest to the child or are familiar to the child. For example, I taught a student who loved animals. A quick trip to the zoo with my camera and the picture book was complete! We would "read" the book by naming the animal in each photo—no words—just photos. I've made other books of farm equipment, dinosaurs, types of cars—anything will work if it is motivating and interesting to the child!

Why It Works!

Because My Picture Book incorporates a child's special interests, the child's attention to the book is often greater than it might be to a book that holds no interest for him or her. The pictures can be changed to build new vocabulary as the child's interests change. Words can also be added to the pictures if desired.

Materials Needed

- ❑ A small photo album
- ❑ Pictures or photographs of the child's special interests or familiar items

ENVIRONMENTAL PRINT BOOK
ACTIVITY

What It Is

An Environmental Print Book is a strategy for early vocabulary building. The book contains photos of familiar labels, logos, and signs that a child encounters frequently in daily life.

Why It Works!

A child will recognize the "golden arches" of McDonald's long before he can read the word "McDonald's" in print. An Environmental Print Book allows a child to "read" and enjoy his favorite labels, logos, and signs in a book format.

Materials Needed

- ❑ A small photo album
- ❑ Pictures or photographs of familiar labels from food products, store logos, and community signs

Ideas for Use

An adult can "read" the book to the child or the child can "read" to the adult—either way is great! You may even find the child picking up the book and reading to himself—even better!! Some people even use the pictures in an Environmental Print Book as a communication tool to help a child understand the errands to be run that day, the groceries to be purchased, etc.

WORD WALL
ACTIVITY

What It Is

A Word Wall can be seen in many elementary school classrooms. It is a collection of words posted on a wall or other surface, in full view of the students. Many times, the word is accompanied by a picture to illustrate the meaning of the word. A word-wall usually consists of words children frequently encounter in their reading; often word wall words are those that do not follow traditional phonetic spelling patterns.

Why It Works!

A Word Wall can be used as a visual reference when reading or writing or for reinforcing vocabulary. The pictures help "cement" the meaning of the words in the minds of the students.

Materials Needed

- ❑ A place to display the word wall (some teachers use the side of a piece of furniture, a portable chart stand, a "science fair-type" display board—anything goes!)
- ❑ Pictures with corresponding words

Ideas for Use

If you introduce the words gradually and discuss them in context, it may help students remember each word and meaning. You could add words a few times a week, by having students pick them out of a grab bag, or via some other engaging and memorable activity.

One of my favorite activities to use with a word wall is called "Flash a Word." Begin by turning off the lights. Using a flashlight, point the light at a word on the wall. See if the children can read the word, tell what it means—whatever your purpose. You can even turn this into a game by allowing a child to "be the teacher" and shine the flashlight on a different word for one of his classmates to read.

See the "Use the Clues" strategy in the Building Comprehension section for another activity to use with the word wall.

Some Ideas for Word Wall Themes

All About Me
Animals
Around the Globe
Around the House
Around Town
Clothing
Community Helpers
Dinosaurs
Fall
Families
Farm
Feelings
Food and Nutrition
Friends
Holidays and Celebrations
Music
Nature
Night and Day
Space
Sports and Games
Spring
Summer
Toys and Hobbies
Transportation and Vehicles
Under the Big Top
Under the Sea
Winter
Zoo Animals

The Picture Communication Symbols ©1981–2010 by Mayer-Johnson LLC. All Rights Reserved Worldwide. Used with permission. Boardmaker™ is a trademark of Mayer-Johnson LLC.

PRINTABLE TOOLS ON THE CD

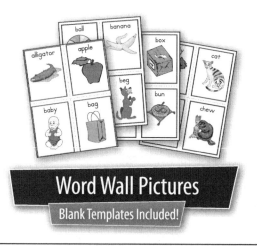

Word Wall Pictures
Blank Templates Included!

THEMATIC WORD WALL
ACTIVITY

What It Is

The Thematic Word Wall is a variation on the word wall strategy often used in classrooms. Words are posted on a wall or other surface, in full view of the students. The vocabulary for the wall consists of words related to the thematic unit being studied.

Why It Works!

The Thematic Word Wall increases a child's vocabulary with theme-specific words. The pictures help "cement" the meaning of the words in the minds of the students.

Materials Needed

❑ A place to display the word wall
❑ Pictures with corresponding words

Ideas for Use

Try to incorporate vocabulary from different parts of speech, not just nouns. Include verbs, adjectives, even some "commenting-type" words, such as "Mmmm" (on a thematic wall involving food), "Brrr" (on a thematic wall involving winter), etc.

Some Ideas for Thematic Word Wall Vocabulary

A Winter/Holiday Theme		
A	avalanche	angel
B	boots	brrr
C	chilly	chimney
D	December	dreidel
E	earmuffs	evergreen
F	fireplace	frozen
G	gloves	garland
H	holiday	hibernate
I	icicle	igloo
J	January	jacket
K	Kwanzaa	kids
L	lights	letter (to Santa)
M	mittens	mistletoe
N	nutcracker	North Pole
O	open	ornaments
P	parka	polar bear
Q	quilt	quiet
R	reindeer	ribbon
S	snowman	snowflake
T	toboggan	turtleneck
U	unwrap	underwear (long!)
V	visitor	vacation
W	winter	weather
X	Xmas	x-tra days off school
Y	yule log	yawn
Z	zipper	zero (degrees)

Around Town Theme		
A	ambulance	alley
B	barber	bridge
C	car	corner
D	doghouse	doctor
E	elevator	exit
F	firetruck	factory
G	grocer	garden
H	hydrant	hospital
I	inside	intersection
J	jogger	janitor
K	kids	kite
L	library	license plate
M	mail carrier	museum
N	neighborhood	nurse
O	open	office
P	park	policeman
Q	quarter	question
R	restroom	restaurant
S	stop sign	sidewalk
T	taxi	traffic light
U	umbrella	U-turn
V	village	veterinarian
W	water fountain	window
X	x-ray	x-tra cheese
Y	yard sale	yield
Z	zoo	zookeeper

Food Theme - Liberties with the X!		FIll in Your Own Theme	
A	apple	artichoke	A		
B	banana	broccoli	B		
C	cookie	carrot	C		
D	donut	dinner	D		
E	egg	eggplant	E		
F	french fries	fruit	F		
G	grapefruit	gravy	G		
H	hot dog	honey	H		
I	ice cream	ice cube	I		
J	jellybean	juice	J		
K	ketchup	kiwi	K		
L	lemonade	lettuce	L		
M	muffin	mustard	M		
N	noodles	nectarine	N		
O	oatmeal	olive	O		
P	pizza	popcorn	P		
Q	quiche	quince	Q		
R	raisins	raspberry	R		
S	sandwich	salad	S		
T	tomato	turkey	T		
U	upside-down cake	ugli fruit	U		
V	vegetable	vanilla wafers	V		
W	walnut	watermelon	W		
X	x-tra crispy chicken	x-tra large pizza	X		
Y	yam	yogurt	Y		
Z	zucchini	Zweiback	Z		

AUDIO CARD READER
ACTIVITY

What It Is

An audio card reader is a commercially available audio-visual device that can be used to help children see and hear words at the same time. The system is comprised of a playback unit and audio cards with a magnetic strip at the bottom. A word, phrase, or sentence can be printed on the card. Then, the printed text can be recorded onto the magnetic strip in much the same manner as a cassette recorder works. The card can then be played through the unit, and the device will "speak" the recorded track. I like to have the children record the track sometimes, too, so that they can hear their own voices played back as they run the card through. You may be familiar with the Language Master product, a specific type of audio card reader found in many schools and available from www.drakeed.com, as well as from many educational supply stores and catalogs.

Why It Works!

For learning vocabulary, children with ASD quite often have a strong auditory sense in addition to their visual learning strength. This audio card reader provides input in both of those areas and helps to "cement" the target word in the mind of the learner.

Materials Needed

❑ An audio card reader
❑ Magnetic cards for recording text (pre-printed or write-on cards)
❑ Illustrations, if you wish, to accompany the text and provide an additional visual prompt

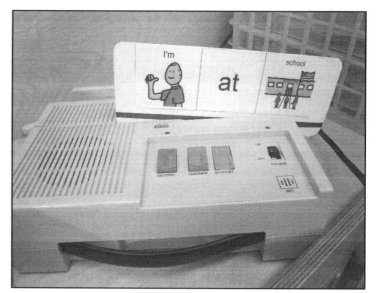

ONE WORD TEXT
ACTIVITY

What It Is

One Word Text is a simple book that matches single words to simple pictures of that word. Any combination of matching words and pictures can be used.

Why It Works!

The One Word Text strategy is a simple strategy for introducing a child to words without extraneous, potentially distracting material on the page. The picture cues provide a visual referent to help the child connect the word to the picture.

Materials Needed

- ❏ One Word Picture Pages
- ❏ Clearly printed words that match each picture
- ❏ Velcro® dots (optional)
- ❏ A method for binding or containing all of the pages

Ideas for Use

To make the book more interactive, place the word on a strip of cardstock that is affixed to the picture page with a Velcro® dot. All of the words can be removed from the book before reading with the child and the child can attempt to match the word to the picture—after a little familiarity with the text, of course! (I like to keep my word cards in a zipped sandwich bag attached to the front cover of the book. The child can then remove all of the word cards and match them to the picture pages as he reads.)

For children who need a bit more cueing before being able to match the words to the pictures independently, you can have the word printed on the picture page in addition to being duplicated on separate word cards. The child can then match the word card to the same word printed on the page.

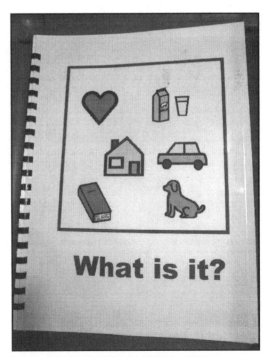

The Picture Communication Symbols ©1981–2010 by Mayer-Johnson LLC. All Rights Reserved Worldwide.
Used with permission. Boardmaker™ is a trademark of Mayer-Johnson LLC.

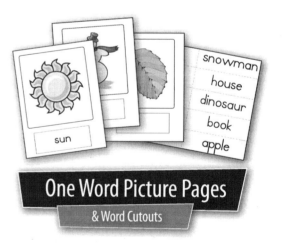

PICTURE ME READING!©

ACTIVITY

What It Is

Picture Me Reading!© is a line of commercial products that teaches the letters of the alphabet and the 220 high frequency sight words from the Dolch sight word list.

The product that I have used most frequently is the Dolch word flash cards. On each card is a printed sight word. Embedded within the printed word is a picture cue, a simple line drawing, to help children visualize the word meaning and remember the "look" of the word. A sentence prompt is also included for each word to help auditory learners remember the meaning of the word through a little "story" format.

Why It Works!

Flash cards are a visual tool that can be used for learning sight word vocabulary. I have found that the additional visual cue, the line drawing, helps children with autism understand the meaning of the word more clearly, since some words (e.g., "for," "both") don't always have a concrete, visual meaning (e.g., "apple," "monkey"). In addition, the 220 Dolch words comprise 60–85% of the text in children's early reading materials, so proficiency in them helps build not only vocabulary, but also fluency and comprehension.

Materials Needed

❑ Picture Me Reading! products can be purchased from:

"Picture Me Reading!"
3899 Kenwood Drive
Spring Valley, CA 91977-1024
Phone or fax: (619) 462-3938/(800) 235-6822
www.picturemereading.com

Picture Me Reading!© Pictograph Samples

I

© 1994, "Picture Me Reading!"

you

© 1994, "Picture Me Reading!"

jump

© 1994, "Picture Me Reading!"

we

© 1994, "Picture Me Reading!"

run

© 1994, "Picture Me Reading!"

up

© 1994, "Picture"
Me Reading!

can

© 1994, "Picture Me Reading!"

down

© 1994, "Picture Me Reading!"

and

© 1994, "Picture Me Reading!"

fast

© 1994, "Picture Me Reading!"

Dolch Sight Word List

Preprimer	Primer	First	Second	Third
a	all	after	always	about
and	am	again	around	better
away	are	an	because	bring
big	at	any	been	carry
blue	ate	as	before	clean
can	be	ask	best	cut
come	black	by	both	done
down	brown	could	buy	draw
find	but	every	call	drink
for	came	fly	cold	eight
funny	did	from	does	fall
go	do	give	don't	far
help	eat	going	fast	full
hers	four	had	first	got
I	get	has	five	grow
in	good	her	found	hold
is	has	him	gave	hot
it	he	how	goes	hurt
jump	into	just	green	if
little	like	know	its	keep
look	must	let	made	kind
make	new	live	many	laugh
me	no	may	off	light
my	now	of	or	long
not	on	old	pull	much
one	our	once	read	myself
play	out	open	right	never
red	please	over	sing	only
run	pretty	put	sit	own

Preprimer	Primer	First	Second	Third
said	ran	round	sleep	pick
see	ride	some	tell	seven
the	saw	stop	their	shall
three	say	take	these	show
to	she	thank	those	six
two	so	them	upon	small
up	soon	then	us	start
we	that	think	use	ten
yellow	there	walk	very	today
you	they	where	wash	together
	this	when	which	try
	too		why	warm
	under		wish	
	want		work	
	was		would	
	well		write	
	went		your	
	what			
	white			
	who			
	will			
	with			
	yes			

WORD WEBS
ACTIVITY

What It Is

A word web is a type of graphic organizer that helps children learn vocabulary associated with parts of objects. In the center of the web is an illustration. Surrounding the illustration are text boxes and lines pointing to different parts of the illustration. The vocabulary words for each of the illustrated parts can be placed on the web to depict the name of each part.

Why It Works!

Word webs provide not only a visual tool for learning vocabulary associated with parts of objects, but also provide a conceptual tool for helping children understand the relationship and organization of parts to a whole. The vocabulary words tend to be less abstract when placed with the illustration. Additionally, children with ASD often have difficulty generalizing the meanings of words. They may learn the word "neck" in the context of their own bodies, but have difficulty realizing that the long neck on a dinosaur is also a "neck." Word webs can help students transfer their learning to different contexts.

Materials Needed

- ❑ The Word Web Picture Pages from the CD, or your own pictures plus corresponding text boxes for the targeted vocabulary
- ❑ A system for children to label each text box with the correct vocabulary (see ideas for use below)

Ideas for Use

Children can place pre-printed word cards on the text boxes and affix with Velcro® or they can write the vocabulary word in the text box. Some children may need a word bank to be able to recall the correct vocabulary word choices.

I also like to use illustrations from stories that we are reading as the center point of a word web. Children can then label the items in the illustration, or work on a particular language skill, such as prepositional phrases, by labeling the web with targeted vocabulary.

Word Web Sample

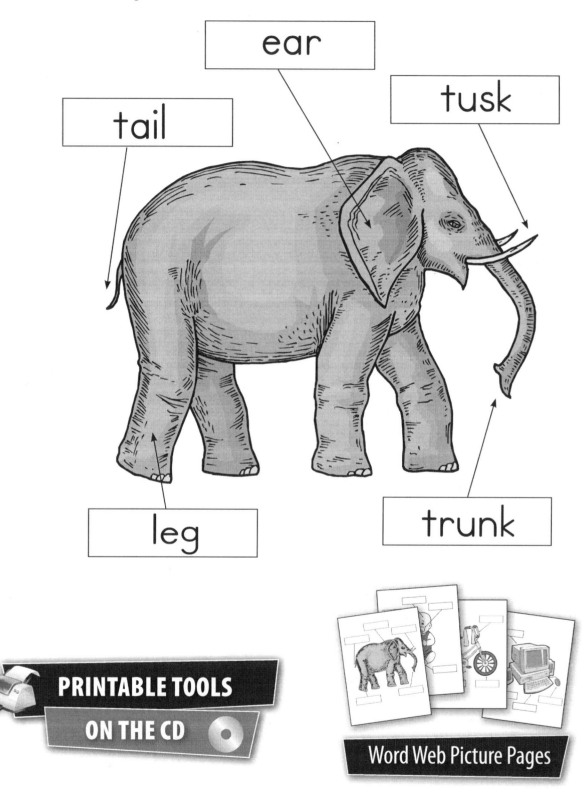

What It Is

In a list poem, every line contains one word or phrase related to the topic of the poem. Students generate the lines of the poem by coming up with vocabulary words related to the topic of the poem. I like to create a large shape of the object that is the topic of our list poem and have my students generate words that we will write in the shape (see examples below and on the next page).

A list poem can be written about any topic—the possibilities are endless!

Why It Works!

A list poem is an engaging, simple, visual strategy for helping students learn and generate vocabulary words related to a topic. It doesn't matter whether the list is comprised of words all starting with a certain letter or word (as in the snowman example) or whether the poem is a collection of different kinds of words related to a topic (as in the dinosaur example)—you set the criteria depending on the needs and abilities of your students.

Materials Needed

❑ The List Poem Pictures from the CD, or your own blank shape to write the poem on (either a large shape to do as a group, or individual sheets for students to create their own)

❑ That's about it!

SNOW!

Snowman
Snowsuit
Snowstorm
Snowflake
Snow Angel
Snowball
Snow Shovel
Snow Boots

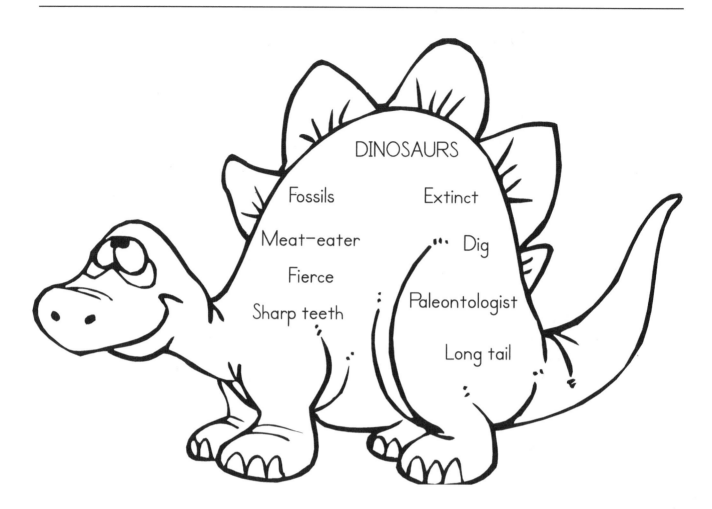

DINOSAURS

Fossils   Extinct

Meat-eater   Dig

Fierce

Sharp teeth   Paleontologist

                   Long tail

PRINTABLE TOOLS

ON THE CD

List Poem Pictures

Ready for words!

COMPREHENSION

COMPREHENSION

What is comprehension?

Comprehension is making meaning from text. Readers construct meaning when they engage in intentional thinking as they read—tapping background knowledge, making personal connections, questioning, and problem-solving.

Comprehension also involves monitoring strategies—good readers use strategies to help them become aware of their level of understanding of the text. Good readers re-read. They simplify and summarize. They ask questions in their head as they read. They ask questions after reading to clarify their understanding.

Why is comprehension important to reading success?

"Comprehension is the reason for reading. If readers can read the words but do not understand what they are reading, they are not really reading." [1]

Reading words without making meaning is like eating without tasting: you are going through the motions, but no enjoyment or fulfillment is derived from the experience.

Additionally, much of the time, we read for information. We read to find out how to do something. We read to understand a topic. We read to explore new worlds. Without understanding what we read, we read for nothing.

How do typically developing young children demonstrate comprehension?

Even the youngest children can demonstrate reading comprehension skills. Early on, children ask questions about characters or events in a text. They may relate their own personal experiences to the occurrences in a story. They may make connections among several stories they have read. They may look back or ahead at illustrations to review or make predictions about what will happen in the story. When they don't understand, young children may ask questions to clarify meaning.

How do young children with ASD struggle with comprehension?

Many times I hear, "He can read the words, but he doesn't understand what he's reading." Children with autism are often strong word-callers, recognizing and naming many words in a text. However, when teachers attempt to discover what the child has

[1] (2001). Armbruster, B., Lehr, F., and Osborn, J. Adler, C. (ed.) Put Reading First: The Research Building Blocks for Teaching Children to Read.

understood from the text, the child may be unable to effectively display his level of understanding. Difficulties with reading comprehension are strongly linked to receptive and expressive language comprehension deficits in students with ASD. It becomes difficult, then, to determine whether the child is comprehending the text but just can't articulate the meaning or whether the child is unable to make meaning from the text at all. In some cases, even, the child may have created meaning from the text, but lacks the needed communication skills to effectively process any questions being asked of him.

Additionally, because of the concrete learning strengths of many children with ASD, they may have difficulty creating abstract connections with the text. Making predictions, drawing conclusions, and visualizing events from a text may present challenges. They may have a limited amount of background knowledge or have difficulty using their background knowledge to make connections with the events or information in the text.

Children with ASD characteristically are challenged by a lack of social understanding and "theory of mind"—the ability to take the perspective of another person and recognize their emotions, interests, and motivations. This area of deficit, then, affects their ability to understand and relate to characters in fictional text.

Additionally, auditory processing difficulties may affect the reading comprehension abilities of many children with ASD. If you think about it, good readers can "hear" themselves read in their heads. They are able to "listen to" their reading and process the information as they read silently. However, for many children with ASD, difficulties with auditory processing may affect their level of comprehension, no matter how fluently they are reading. The thought processes behind the fluency are affected by their auditory processing challenges.

How can comprehension be developed?

Students with autism may need explicit instruction to learn how to comprehend text. They need to see how connections are made. They need concrete learning opportunities. They need modeling to see how "comprehending" looks. They need lots of repetition and practice to internalize new techniques.

Adults or good peer readers can help children with ASD improve their comprehension skills. Good readers can model their own comprehension processes. Model by thinking aloud. Verbalize the questions that are running through your head: *"Hmmm, I wonder what made the character cry?"* Verbalize your personal connections: *"I remember when I went to the zoo. I liked the hippos the best, but they sure were stinky!"*

Help students begin to make connections themselves by building their background knowledge. Help them relate the content of what they are reading to a personal experience. In some cases, it may be easier to work first on comprehension of nonfiction text since it tends to be more concrete and literal than fiction.

Help them understand character motivations by again relating to personal experiences. Provide direct instruction in understanding feelings and emotions. Help them form pictures in their heads by drawing, if need be, what is being read. Show them what it means to "think" and form a picture in your mind. Readers who can visualize what they read generally remember what they read better than readers who do not visualize as they read.

Comprehension is a challenge for students with autism spectrum disorders. Your challenge, as teachers and parents of those children, is to help them acquire these essential skills so that they may reap the benefits of a life filled with reading success!

LANGUAGE EXPERIENCE STORY
ACTIVITY

What It Is

A Language Experience Story is a story based on personal experience. Preschool teachers write Language Experience Stories with their young students—particularly as thank-you notes after a field trip or other such adventure. To write a Language Experience Story, first you have to have an experience! For example, a class or family may take a trip to the zoo. Following the experience, an adult talks with the child about what occurred during the trip. The adult writes the child's words exactly—hopefully in sentence format! This allows the student to see and hear the words and helps to develop the sight/sound relationship needed for effective reading skills. After writing the story, you and the child can read and re-read it to recall the series of events that were experienced.

Why It Works!

Because students with autism often have restricted interests, one of the best methods for engaging them with a text is to use their personal experiences and interests. Language Experience Stories are powerful tools for tapping into background knowledge and personal experiences of children with autism—strategies that are essential to comprehending other texts as their reading skills develop. Language Experience Stories help young children combine literacy skills, language skills, and concept development related to real events.

Materials Needed

- ❏ An experience!
- ❏ Something to record the experience on (paper, poster board, computer, etc.) to create a story
- ❏ Illustrations or photographs to make the text even more meaningful

A Handy Tip

Children with ASD tend to live in the present, so recalling and describing past experiences may be a challenge for them. Even if they remember specific details about the trip, it may be difficult for them to put those memories into words. So take pictures and take notes during the trip! A photo diary can provide visual cues and foster more effective and relevant communication.

Language Experience Story Sample

Our Trip to the Zoo

We went to the zoo.

We saw lots of animals.

The hippos were fat and stinky.

The giraffe was tall.

He was eating leaves from a tall tree.

We saw monkeys.

They were swinging and playing.

We saw a zebra.

He was black and white.

We got some ice cream.

Then we went home.

BOOK BOX
ACTIVITY

What It Is

A Book Box is literally a box of props that can be used to depict the events in a book. For example, my Book Box for the book, *If You Give a Mouse a Cookie* by Laura Joffe Numeroff, contains a stuffed animal mouse, a pretend cookie, a pretend glass of milk. A Book Box can be made for simple, one-word-on-a-page books, or for books with a more traditional story, depending on the needs and abilities of the child.

Why It Works!

The Book Box props provide concrete representations of elements from the text. I use the Book Box while reading a text and also after I read, to retell or "act out" the events in the text.

The concrete items help kinesthetic and visual learners form a stronger understanding of what the words and illustrations on the page are describing. The Book Box can also be a tool for determining a child's comprehension level, especially for children who need prompts to use their language skills.

Materials Needed

- ❑ A book
- ❑ A collection of props to portray the characters, events, or setting in the book
- ❑ A box or other container to hold the props (and the book, if you wish)

 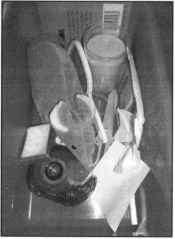

SIMON SAYS...BOOK
ACTIVITY

What It Is

A Simon Says Book is a simple, predictable text that anyone can write! It is intended to be read independently by the child, and used to assess his level of comprehension. Any topic can be used for the action text lines—the sample I've included uses different action verbs and body parts as the featured vocabulary.

Why It Works!

Because the Simon Says book is predictable, students can attain a comfort level with reading it independently. However, after the "Simon says …" repetitive line, the subsequent lines of text change with each page. The child's level of comprehension can be assessed by listening to him read the action line and perform the intended action. Visual prompts are purposely left out of the action line so that no additional cues as to the meaning of the words are provided to the student.

Materials Needed

❏ The Simon Says Book Samples on the CD, and/or any text that you write that fits your child's reading level

❏ A book or other method for binding the pages together

Other Topic Ideas

✓ Simon says … find the square (and other shapes you may have in front of the student).

✓ Simon says … make a cow sound (and other animal sounds).

✓ Simon says … name something that starts with A (and other letters of the alphabet)

✓ Simon says … put the spoon in the cup
(and other directions with items
you have in front of the student).

A Handy Tip

Check out www.barebooks.com. They have all kinds of blank books for extremely reasonable prices—you can make your own very sturdy, professional-looking book using their products. They even carry blank board books. The book in the photo is a Bare Book product that I used to create my Simon Says book.

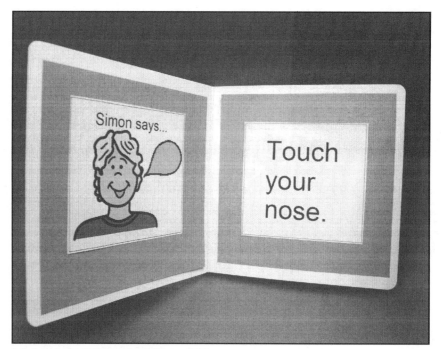

The Picture Communication Symbols ©1981–2010 by Mayer-Johnson LLC. All Rights Reserved Worldwide. Used with permission. Boardmaker™ is a trademark of Mayer-Johnson LLC.

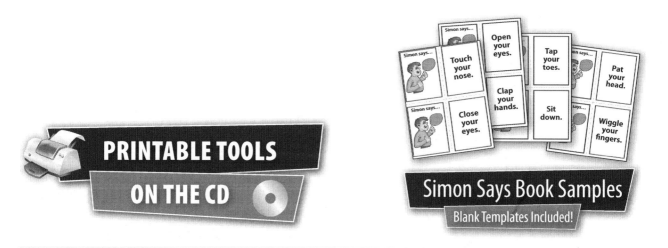

TEXT-PICTURE MATCH
ACTIVITY

What It Is

Text-Picture Match is a strategy for checking a child's comprehension when reading independently. A simple text and corresponding illustrations are needed. However, the illustrations should be separate from the text, as students will need to match them to the correct line of text to demonstrate their understanding of what they have read. I usually write my own stories based on the child's abilities and which pictures are avaiable.

Why It Works!

Like the Simon Says book, Text-Picture Match contains no visual cues right on the page of text to clue the student in to the meaning of the text. A student's comprehension is checked, however, when he matches the correct illustration to the corresponding line of text. The illustration, when matched correctly, helps children realize that the words they have read have meaning.

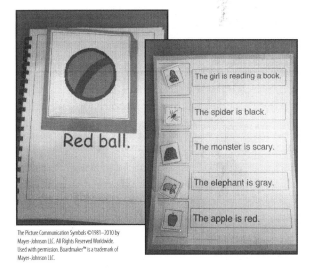

The Picture Communication Symbols ©1981–2010 by Mayer-Johnson LLC. All Rights Reserved Worldwide. Used with permission. Boardmaker™ is a trademark of Mayer-Johnson LLC.

Materials Needed

- ❏ A text with simple sentences
- ❏ Illustrations separate from the text that can be matched to the correct line of text
- ❏ Velcro® or other method of attaching the illustrations to the text pages
- ❏ A binder or other method of binding the book

PRINTABLE TOOLS ON THE CD

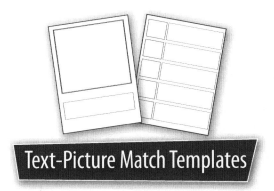

Text-Picture Match Templates

COVER PICTURE PREDICTION
ACTIVITY

What It Is

Good readers, even beginning readers, use reading strategies to help them make meaning from text. One reading strategy that you can help children learn to use is that of making predictions. Predicting can be a rather abstract strategy. However, you can make it more concrete for your students. Think for a moment … when you examine a children's book, before you read an excerpt, how do you determine what it might be about? You look at the title, you look at the pictures, etc. The Cover Picture Prediction strategy teaches children to use cover illustrations to make a prediction about the book's content.

Why It Works!

The Cover Picture Prediction strategy makes what could be an abstract concept more literal for students. It teaches them to look at the cover and name what they see in order to draw a conclusion about the book's content. It teaches the "language" of predicting and focuses on a student's visual learning strengths.

Materials Needed

- ❏ A book
- ❏ The Cover Picture Prediction Form from the CD
- ❏ Picture cues, as needed, to prompt your students' language

Ideas for Use

Prior to reading a text, ask students, "What do you think this story might be about?" Instruct them to look at the illustrations on the cover and name what they see. This strategy can be differentiated for the different levels of your students: some students may name what they see in the cover illustration and match a picture choice to the picture on the cover; others may be able to articulate their prediction in a sentence using the sentence starter prompts, with no picture choices.

I like to have the students attach their prediction (the picture cue or the sentence starter) to the cover of the book, to further demonstrate that predictions can come from what you see. (I put a Velcro strip on the cover of some of my books so they're ready for this strategy!)

After reading, as a follow-up to check the accuracy of the prediction, you can re-visit the Cover Picture Prediction and ask, "You thought this book might be about _____. Were you correct?"

Note: In the example shown in the photograph, one student could have made the prediction that the book would be about a snowball; another student could have made the prediction that the book would be about kids. With this particular book, they would both be right. That could lead to a further discussion—how was this book about kids AND a snowball?

PICTURE WALK
ACTIVITY

What It Is

A picture walk is another strategy for teaching students how to make predictions. Before reading a story, have students flip through the book, noting the illustrations on each page—"walk" through the pictures, but don't read the words yet. In the same manner as described in the Cover Picture Prediction strategy, have them state what they see on each page in order to make predictions about what might happen in the story. As with the Cover Picture Prediction, help students see that they should use what they see on the page as a basis for their predictions.

Why It Works!

As with the Cover Picture Prediction strategy, a Picture Walk is a strategy for showing students how to make predictions—how to think about their reading before they read. A Picture Walk can build interest in the story. It also reinforces the strategy of relying on visual cues to help make meaning while reading—a strategy of good readers at all stages. Taking a Picture Walk also helps students become familiar with the story and activate prior knowledge about the subject matter before reading the text.

Materials Needed

- ❏ A book
- ❏ Picture Walk Poem
- ❏ Visual cues as needed

Using the Picture Walk Poem on the CD

This cute poem describes how to take a Picture Walk. I read this poem with my students prior to taking a Picture Walk to remind them how it is done.

PRINTABLE TOOLS
ON THE CD

Picture Walk Poem

Let's take a picture walk,

but do not yell or shout.

Just think about the pictures,

then tell what they're about.

Original source unknown. Thank you to the creative poet, whoever you are!

QUESTION STICKS

ACTIVITY

What It Is

Question Sticks are visual representations to help children understand what question words are asking. Question Sticks can be used to represent the following question words:

Who?   What?
When?   Where?
Why   Which One?

Why It Works!

Because some children with ASD have difficulty processing questions, Question Sticks put the question in a visual format—a format the child may better understand.

The Picture Communication Symbols © 1981–2010 by Mayer-Johnson LLC. All Rights Reserved Worldwide. Used with permission. Boardmaker™ is a trademark of Mayer-Johnson LLC.

Materials Needed

❏ Popsicle® or craft sticks
❏ Question Stick Cue Cards from the CD, laminated and taped to the stick

Ideas for Use

When asking a comprehension question that begins with one of the question words on the sticks, hold up the stick as you ask the question. You may have to remind students of the visual cue on the stick to help them answer the question. For example, "who" usually means a person or character; "which one" means to select from several choices, etc.

PRINTABLE TOOLS
ON THE CD

Question Stick Cue Cards

QUESTION CUES
ACTIVITY

What It Is

Just like Question Sticks, Question Cues are visual representations to help children understand what question words are asking. Question Cues represent the following question words:

Who?	What?
When?	Where?
Why	Which One?

The Picture Communication Symbols ©1981–2010 by Mayer-Johnson LLC. All Rights Reserved Worldwide. Used with permission. Boardmaker™ is a trademark of Mayer-Johnson LLC.

Why It Works!

Question Cues not only put the question word in a visual format but also go a step beyond Question Sticks by providing visual choices to help children who may struggle with language to answer the question being asked. A visual cue to represent the meaning of the question word is provided, as well as three choices of answers to help those who struggle with language to respond to the question.

Materials Needed

- ❑ The Question Cue Pages from the CD, laminated
- ❑ 3 loop Velcro® dots or a small strip of soft Velcro attached to the side of each laminated page
- ❑ A folder, three-ring binder or spiral binder to contain the cues in "book" form
- ❑ Laminated "answer" choices in picture form, related to the text

PRINTABLE TOOLS ON THE CD

Question Cue Pages

USE THE CLUES
ACTIVITY

What It Is

Use the Clues is a strategy for helping students think. The concept of "thinking" is kind of abstract, and many students with ASD have difficulty using verbal cues to create a picture in their minds and "think."

Why It Works!

Use the Clues teaches students to focus on important details and use them to create a picture in their mind of what is being described. This thinking process is explicitly taught as you help the child "rule out" choices that don't correspond with the given clue. Having concrete items in front of the students, helps them see clearly which items do and do not fit the clues. Once your students get the hang of this technique, you can advance to no visual supports, just verbalizing the clues and helping them focus on the important details. This technique helps students paint pictures in their heads as they listen to or read the text, focusing on important details to create an accurate understanding of the text.

Materials Needed

- ❑ A collection of objects or pictures
- ❑ Clues to help students determine the item you are describing (It is probably wise to write out your clues so that they are very clear and systematically rule out certain items each time you give a clue.)
- ❑ Chart paper or somewhere to write the important details from the clues for your students, if you choose to do so

An Example

Pictures or objects to have in view as choices:

- ❑ A red crayon
- ❑ A tomato
- ❑ A red ball
- ❑ A red balloon
- ❑ A teddy bear (not red)
- ❑ An apple

Clues

Say:

"I'm thinking of something that is red." (Rule out the teddy bear.)

"It is red and round." (Rule out the crayon.)

"It is red and round and you can eat it." (Rule out the ball and the balloon.)

"It is red and round and you can eat it and it grows on a tree." (Rule out the tomato.)

"What is it? AN APPLE!"

A Handy Tip

You may wish to write the key words from your clues (red, round, eat it, grows on a tree) so that the students can see as well as hear the clues to use.

THINKING IN PICTURES
ACTIVITY

What It Is

Thinking in Pictures is a strategy for helping children learn how to visualize what they read or hear.

Why It Works!

If you think about it, understanding what it means to "think" is really challenging! Concrete, visual learners, like most children with autism, may need a concrete, visual representation of the abstract concept of thinking. The Thinking in Pictures strategy provides this concrete, visual representation of what it means to think. (This works particularly well for children who are artistic or have some drawing ability.)

Materials Needed

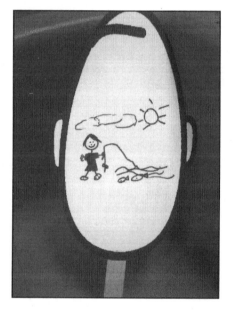

- ❑ A laminated "head"
- ❑ A Popsicle® stick or tongue depressor
- ❑ Tape
- ❑ Dry-erase marker

OR

- ❑ Paper copies of the head
- ❑ Crayons or markers
- ❑ A descriptive portion of text to use as a stimulus for thinking in pictures

Ideas for Use

(This is how I use the materials—you decide what works best for you.)

The children either have laminated heads on sticks or paper copies of the head and tools for drawing (dry-erase markers for drawing on the laminated heads or regular markers or crayons for drawing on the paper copies).

How Do I Teach This Kid to Read?
© 2010 by Kimberly A. Henry. Future Horizons, Inc.

First, I model the thinking process. I read a descriptive excerpt from a text aloud and draw a picture that I am forming in my head as I read. I usually read one line at a time and add to my drawing as I go. I deliberately point out elements that I am drawing and where the clues came from in the text.

Next, I have students practice Thinking in Pictures. I read an excerpt aloud, one line at a time, and have them draw what they hear. I usually have the text printed on poster paper or projected so students can see the text as I read it aloud.

Sometimes, I may need to point out key words that should help them know what to draw. We may need to have conversations like this:

I may begin, "The story says, 'The boy went fishing in the lake.' What does that make you see in your head? Who went fishing?"

The child might answer, "A boy," and then I would underline or highlight the word "boy" in the text to show them the clue that is right there. Then I might say, "Okay, draw a boy."

Then I might ask, "Where did he go fishing?"

The child might answer, "In the lake," and then I would underline or highlight the word "lake" in the text to show them the clue that is right there. Then I might say, "Okay, now draw a lake."

Finally, I might ask, "What does he need to go fishing?"

Some children might have difficulty with this because they lack the background knowledge about fishing and the clue is not "right there" in the text as the others are. I might encourage the children to work together to share their knowledge about fishing, or I might offer two choices: "Do you need a fork to go fishing, or do you need a fishing pole?"

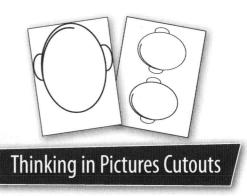

Thinking in Pictures Cutouts

PRINTABLE TOOLS ON THE CD

COMMENT STOP

ACTIVITY

What It Is

Comment Stop is a during-reading strategy for helping students think about their reading. If we are reading a big book or other group text, I mark specific places in the text with Comment Stop cue cards (see sample). When we get to these points in the text, I have students make a comment about what they have read so far. If students are reading individual books, they can use a clothespin or other similar device to clip a Comment Stop cue card to various spots in their text to signal them to stop and make a comment about what they have read.

Why It Works!

The Comment Stop strategy teaches students to use the reading comprehension strategy of thinking aloud. Thinking as they read is a strategy used by good readers to help with comprehension—to make meaning from text, to use fix-up strategies, to sort out confusing parts of a text, etc. During reading, teachers and parents can model their thought processes for children by making comments about the text as they go along. The Comment Stop Commenting Board provides visual cues to give students something to say when they need help generating the language for commenting.

Materials Needed

- ❏ A big book or other text
- ❏ The Comment Stop Cue Cards & Board from the CD, laminated
- ❏ Tape, Velcro®, clothespins, or some other means of attaching the cue cards to your text

The Picture Communication Symbols © 1981–2010 by Mayer-Johnson LLC. All Rights Reserved Worldwide. Used with permission. Boardmaker™ is a trademark of Mayer-Johnson LLC.

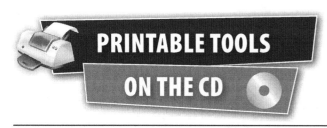

PRINTABLE TOOLS

ON THE CD

Comment Stop Cue Cards & Board

FEELINGS

ACTIVITY

What It Is

Children with ASD have much difficulty understanding social cues and "reading" social situations. They may not realize that a child who is crying is hurt or sad; a person who is laughing is happy; a person who is backing up when another person is talking to them may feel that their personal space is invaded, etc. This lack of social understanding makes relating to storybook characters—their experiences, motivations, and feelings—difficult as well. Direct instruction in what it looks like to be _____ (emotion), what might make someone _____ (emotion), and how others respond to someone who is _____ (emotion) needs to be provided to students. This strategy uses photographs of real people demonstrating various emotions to teach students with ASD to recognize those emotions, understand what might be causing them, and empathize appropriately.

Why It Works!

Pictures, pictures, pictures! This strategy uses real pictures (or even better—real people!) to show what an emotion looks like. It provides direct, explicit, concrete instruction in recognizing and understanding emotions. The more practice a child has with this strategy with concrete, visual cues, the better he will be at transferring his social understanding to what he reads in a text.

Materials Needed

❑ The Feelings Photo Sheets from the CD, and/or other photos of people displaying various emotions (Search the web! You can find all sorts of pictures there—any pictures of the actor Jim Carrey making a face tend to be super-exaggerated and can be good examples of emotions.)

Ideas for Use

You can do any number of things with these emotion photos, depending on the needs and abilities of your students.

✓ Start by showing one photo at a time and having students name the emotion portrayed in the picture. Start with easy, obvious ones—happy, sad, scared, etc.

✓ Ask students to tell you how they KNOW the person is happy, sad, etc. What clues in the photo tell you that (tears, a smile, etc.)? Help them see the essential details that depict the emotion.

✓ Generate a list of situations with students that might cause a person to be happy, sad, etc. Recognizing an emotion in a person's face is a start, but understanding how an experience might cause a certain emotion is a more advanced step.

✓ Tie the emotion photos and lists to actual characters in a story. Read an event that happens to a character and have students decide how that character might be feeling based on what happened.

PRINTABLE TOOLS ON THE CD

Feelings Photo Sheets

IT'S RIGHT THERE

ACTIVITY

What It Is

It's Right There is a strategy for helping students answer comprehension questions about a text. Students sometimes need to be shown that an answer may be "right there" in the text, relatively easy to find, in a sentence very similar to the words used in the comprehension question they are being asked.

Why It Works!

Children with ASD like "black and white," literal, "right" answers. It's Right There helps them see that sometimes, answers are "right there" in the text—they just have to find them. (Sometimes, answers are not "right there"—to help students with this concept that involves more thinking on their own, search the web for "Reading Stances." Some helpful websites are listed below.)

http://www.doe.state.de.us/files/pdf/reading_qarsandstances.pdf
http://www.intercom.net/local/school/sdms/mspap/stances.html
http://www.mcps.k12.md.us/departments/oipd/mspap/reading.html

Materials Needed

- ❏ A simple text
- ❏ Comprehension questions that use practically identical language in the question as is in the original line of text (The Cal Ripken Story & Questions from the CD is a good example of a simple text and appropriate questions.)

Ideas for Use

1. Read a simple text with students. I find that nonfiction works well when first introducing this strategy because it contains more facts and often requires less interpretation.
2. Ask simple, literal comprehension questions, one at a time. Help the students identify the key words in the question. Highlight or circle them for the students so they can see what information they are being asked.

3. Model for students how to find the answer to one of the questions. Show them how you scan the text for the key words from the question. Highlight or circle key words in the text that will help you answer the question. For example, let's assume the text says, "The Boston Red Sox won the World Series in 2004," and the question is, "Who won the World Series in 2004?" The key words from the question might be "won," "World Series," and "2004." Highlight these words both in the question and in the text, and show students how the answer "Boston Red Sox" is *right there* in the text.

Here is a variation on this strategy, using the nursery rhyme "Humpty Dumpty." The questions include:

What is Humpty Dumpty?

Where did he sit?

What happened?

Who came to help him?

Could they put Humpty Dumpty together again?

The questions are simple and are based directly on the text but do not use all of the same language as the text. This is just a different application of the strategy.

The Picture Communication Symbols © 1981–2010 by Mayer-Johnson LLC. All Rights Reserved Worldwide. Used with permission. Boardmaker™ is a trademark of Mayer-Johnson LLC.

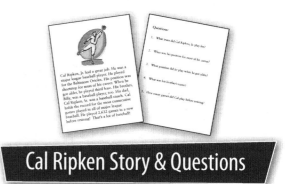

PRINTABLE TOOLS ON THE CD

Cal Ripken Story & Questions

VISUAL ORGANIZERS

ACTIVITY

What It Is

Visual organizers, graphic organizers, webs—they're all the same idea. Visual organizers are basically graphical ways of representing information. There are dozens of visual organizers that can be used for different purposes—organizing details, comparing and contrasting, sequencing events—you name it, there's a visual organizer for it!

Why It Works!

For students with ASD, the visual format aids in their understanding of how pieces of a text fit together—whether it's story elements, a sequence of events, or character traits. Putting the information in a visual format helps students with ASD understand and remember the information.

Materials Needed

❑   A visual organizer of your choosing, depending on the literary concept to be organized

The Visual Organizer Sheets on the CD include:

✓   Story Train—for sequencing events in the beginning, middle, and end of a story

✓   Story Elements—for recording simple statements about what happened in a story—characters, problem or actions, setting

✓   Category Columns—for organizing information based on categories (This one works well with nonfiction. For example, after reading a story or book about migrating animals, in one column you could list animals that travel on land, in another you could list animals that travel on water, and in the final column you could list animals that travel in the air.)

✓   Sequence Chain—for sequencing multiple events in fiction or nonfiction

✓   T-Chart—for comparing two concepts, characters, etc. (for example, Who lives in the jungle? YES—parrot, monkey, etc. NO—cow, cat, etc.)

Visual Organizer Resources

Two of my favorite visual organizer resource books are *Charts for Children* by Judy Nyberg and *Great Graphic Organizers to Use with Any Book!* by Michelle O'Brien-Palmer.

Also, check out www.inspiration.com. Inspiration™ and Kidspiration™ are computer software programs you can use to create visual organizers.

FLUENCY

FLUENCY

What is fluency?

Fluency is the ability to read a text quickly and accurately. A reader's fluency changes with his or her familiarity with the text. For example, you may consider yourself a fluent reader; however, if asked to read from a highly technical text beyond your area of expertise, you may become a non-fluent reader of that text. Students are most likely to be fluent with text that they have read several times and whose words they recognize.

Why is fluency important to reading success?

Fluency is a bridge between word recognition and comprehension. Fluent readers are almost "automatic" readers—they recognize the sounds and words without having to stop and think about them. Because fluent readers do not have to concentrate on decoding the words, they can focus their attention on the meaning behind the words. As they read, fluent readers make connections between the text and their personal experiences and among ideas in the text. Fluency, then, influences comprehension: non-fluent readers experience the text in chopped-up segments, seeing little flow or meaning behind the string of single words. Fluent readers, on the other hand, experience the text as a whole and are able to perceive the meaning behind the words and develop a personal understanding of the author's message.

How do typically developing young children demonstrate fluency?

Even though they are just beginning readers, young children can develop fluency. Adults encourage fluency in young children by modeling fluent reading. Typically developing children demonstrate fluency by listening to a familiar text over and over again and then rereading the story, often with the same speed and inflection as the adult reader. Reading along with a fluent reader or reading along with a taped or computer reading of the text helps young children build fluency skills. An early fluency skill is being able to "sight read" some words. Books with predictable text build fluency in young children, as they read a similar set of words on each page and can anticipate the repetition of each new line.

How do young children with ASD struggle with fluency?

Although young children with autism may recognize many words, they may still struggle with developing fluency. Remember that fluent readers read with expression and meaning; they can use the individual words to help build the "big picture" of the text. Children with autism often miss the "big picture." Because one characteristic of many children with autism is an intense focus on details, they may recognize and enjoy each individual sound or word but miss the story the words are telling. Also, they may recognize the words in the text when presented in isolation, but they may not read the same words fluently when connected in sentences in the text.

In addition, the oral reading of children with ASD may be expressionless. To read with expression, readers must know when to pause appropriately, must know when to change their tone to reflect the emotions of different characters, must know which words to emphasize to provide the most impact. Much of this knowledge is a byproduct of social skill and pragmatic language development—two areas of weakness for many young children with autism. Fluent readers recognize the underlying emotional tones as they read; children with autism often do not.

How can fluency be developed?

Reading fluency can be developed by modeling fluent reading. Read aloud daily to young children. Read with expression. By listening to good models of fluent reading, children learn how a reader's voice can help written text make sense. Change voices to reflect different characters as you read. Help the child understand that there are different speakers with different messages in the text. Make the text come alive!

Additionally, have children engage in repeated oral readings of books that are at their independent level of reading ability—books that are relatively easy for them to read and contain mostly words they know. Model a fluent reading of the text and have the child imitate your speed and inflection—even if it is one line at a time! Provide guidance and feedback as the child reads—encourage the different voices they use to portray the characters, and react to their expression and emphasis of meaningful words. Laugh. Cry. Be scared. Show them that reading has meaning and emotion!

READ TO ME

ACTIVITY

What It Is

One of the simplest ways to increase reading fluency is to read to a child.

Why It Works!

The development of literacy begins at an early age. Reading aloud to your child may be the single most important strategy for developing these early literacy skills. Reading aloud builds listening and concentration skills and helps a child begin to process words and language. By listening to models of fluent reading, children develop an understanding of pacing and expressive reading. Reading favorite stories over and over again fosters curiosity and a love for reading—keep in mind that the experiences and emotions that children associate with reading during their early years can and will affect their feelings toward reading as adolescents and adults.

Materials Needed

- ❑ Books
- ❑ A child, an adult, and a lap!

Tips for Reading Aloud

- ❑ Select reading materials that interest your child
- ❑ Select a variety of texts—fiction, nonfiction, poetry
- ❑ Vary your tone of voice and use different voices for different characters as you read
- ❑ Be sure to emphasize the punctuation. For example, read excitedly a sentence that ends in an exclamation point. Let the pitch of your voice rise when reading a question.
- ❑ Create a personalized book about your child. Children love to be the center of attention—what better way than in a story!
- ❑ Track the print with your finger when you read. Have your child turn the page.
- ❑ If you don't feel comfortable reading a text, practice it before reading to your child so that your reading is more fluent.

ECHO READING
ACTIVITY

What It Is

Echo reading is a strategy in which two readers take turns reading aloud from the same text. One reader reads a portion of text, and then the second reader "echoes" or re-reads the same portion of text. Echo reading can be done with an adult and child or two children. Sometimes more fluent readers are paired with less fluent readers; sometimes two equally fluent readers echo read.

Why It Works!

Echo reading allows one reader to model fluent reading for the other reader. By listening to the first reading, the second reader hears the pronunciation of words he may not recognize and hears the text read with proper phrasing and expression.

Materials Needed

- ❏ A simple text
- ❏ Two readers

Ideas for Use

For very beginning readers, try echo reading with just one word at a time. Cue the child to repeat after you by saying "your turn" or "now you say it." When the child can correctly imitate one word, increase to multi-word phrases, simple sentences, and finally, multi-sentence readings.

PREDICTABLE TEXT
ACTIVITY

What It Is

Predictable or repetitive texts are books that contain words, phrases, or sentences that are repeated throughout the text or are changed only slightly throughout the text. Often, predictable texts will make use of rhyme as well. Patterns may also be built throughout the text. For example, perhaps one of the most famous predictable texts, *Brown Bear, Brown Bear, What Do You See?*, by Bill Martin, Jr., builds a pattern of each new animal seeing something new as the pages turn. The same basic sentence is used on each page, with only the name and color of the new animal changing as the text progresses.

Why It Works!

Predictable texts allow even the most novice of readers to participate in the reading of the text, especially after becoming familiar with the pattern or repetition. Children see the same words over and over again and gain comfort with the predictability of knowing what word to expect next. Predictable text that employs a sentence pattern such as that described in *Brown Bear*, above, also provides opportunities for language play and creativity beyond the author's actual text (see ideas for use below).

Materials Needed

❏ Any predictable or repetitive text (see book titles on following pages)

Ideas for Use

1. Predictable texts work well for choral reading—reading lines of text together with a group or reading partner. Depending on the structure of the text, the more experienced reader could read any novel lines and the group or partner could chime in with the repetitive line(s).

2. You can create your own predictable texts, tailored to the special interests or experiences of your child by "borrowing" some of the repetitive lines from a favorite predictable book. In my preschool classroom, my students and I make a class book using the *Brown Bear* pattern: instead of animals, we use the students in the class (e.g., Johnny, Johnny, who do you see? I see Kayla looking at me.). This helps them learn their friends' names at the beginning of the school year.

3. Predictable texts can also be used as a vocabulary building strategy. Again, consider *Brown Bear*. Having the child name each new animal that is introduced and what they see provides an opportunity to practice recognizing and naming new vocabulary.

Predictable Text Titles

Note: This is certainly not an all-inclusive list, but it will get you started with some popular titles.

Are You My Mother?
    by P. D. Eastman

The Big Wide-Mouthed Frog
    by Ana Martin Larranaga

Brown Bear, Brown Bear, What Do You See?
    by Bill Martin, Jr.

The Cat Sat on the Mat
    by Alice Cameron

Chicka Chicka Boom Boom
    by Bill Martin, Jr. and John Archambault

Do You Want to Be My Friend?
    by Eric Carle

The Earth Is Good: A Chant in Praise of Nature
    by Michael DeMunn

Five Little Monkeys Jumping on the Bed
    by Eileen Christelow

Good Night, Gorilla
    by Peggy Rathmann

Goodnight Moon
   by Margaret Wise Brown

Have You Seen My Cat?
   by Eric Carle

Here Are My Hands
   by Bill Martin, Jr. and John Archambault

If You Give a Moose a Muffin
   by Laura Joffe Numeroff

If You Give a Mouse a Cookie
   by Laura Joffe Numeroff

I Know an Old Lady Who Swallowed a Fly
   by Colin Hawkins and Jacqui Hawkins

Is Your Mama a Llama?
   by Deborah Guarino

It Looked Like Spilt Milk
   by Charles G. Shaw

Jesse Bear, What Will You Wear?
   by Nancy W. Carlstrom

Jump, Frog, Jump!
   by Robert Kalan

The Little Old Lady Who Was Not Afraid of Anything
   by Linda Williams

The Little Red Hen
   by Paul Galdone

Mrs. Wishy-Washy
   by Joy Cowley

The Napping House
   by Audrey Wood

Polar Bear, Polar Bear, What Do You Hear?
   by Bill Martin, Jr.

Sleep, Little One, Sleep
   by Marion Dane Bauer

This Train
   by Paul Collicutt

What the Sun Sees/What the Moon Sees
   by Nancy Tafuri

Wheels on the Bus
   by Raffi

Where's Spot?
   by Eric Hill

Who Hops?
   by Katie Davis

Whose Ears?
   by Jeannette Rowe

PACING BOARD

ACTIVITY

What It Is

A pacing board is a visual cuing system which uses dots, picture cues, or word cues on a piece of foam board or other portable, flat surface to help children increase the length of their spoken language.

Why It Works!

By representing visually each element of the sentence or phrase, children can "see" the number of words they are expected to say. The concrete, visual cue helps them understand more clearly that there are distinct words on the page.

Materials Needed

- ❏ A sturdy board or other surface
- ❏ Stickers, dots, pictures, and/or words to represent each element of the phrase or sentence
- ❏ A text with short phrases or sentences (Repetitive or predictable text is best. Lakeshore® makes great books—pictured at right—that I use all the time!)

Ideas for Use

To use a pacing board, you should model the sentence or phrase first, pointing to each spot on the pacing board as each word is read. I like to place my pacing board right under the line of text to show children that my number of "spots" matches the number of words in the sentence. For example, when reading "Go, dog, go," point to the first spot as you say "go," the second spot as you say "dog," and the third spot as you say "go." Then the child should imitate your reading, also pointing to each spot as he reads a word.

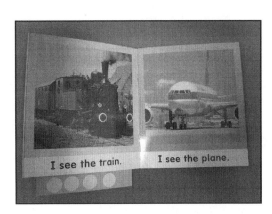

Depending on the child, you may need to place your hand over his hand to guide him to point to each dot as he reads. To build speed, you can take another turn with the same sentence, increasing speed this time and encouraging the child to imitate the new speed.

A Handy Tip

You can use a special interest of your child's (such as animals or racing cars) to serve as the markers on the board. The pictures or stickers may draw your child's attention to the board, but be careful that he does not focus too much on the pictures themselves and become unable to use the board for its intended purpose.

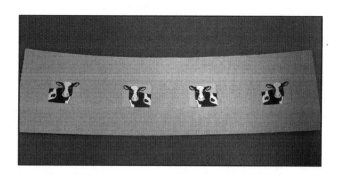

Another Handy Tip

To get the most use out of your pacing boards, make them two-sided. Place three spots on one side and four spots on the other side to allow the same board to be used for text containing both three and four words. I have several pacing boards—2/3, 3/4, 4/5, etc.

Thanks to speech pathologists everywhere who use the pacing board as a strategy for building multiword combinations and increasing sentence length in people with speech difficulties.

SENTENCE BUILDER
ACTIVITY

What It Is

A Sentence Builder is an interactive "flip" book (much like the Magic Words Book described in the section on Phonemic Awareness). Each book contains one sentence "stem" and multiple options for completing the sentence. For example, the sentence stem "I like to eat _____" can be completed with any number of words (e.g., apples, ice cream, pizza, etc.). The sentence stem is written on the back card of the book, with flip cards to complete the sentence layered on the top of the stem (see photo below).

Why It Works!

As with Magic Word Books, Sentence Builders are visual and predictable. The same stem is read repeatedly, with different words completing the sentence. This repetition builds fluency as children gain competence and familiarity with the stem words and just have to focus on the new "flip" word(s) each time they read the sentence.

Materials Needed

You can use the Sentence Builder Starters on the CD to create a landscape flip book, bound on the right-hand side with spiral binding or binder rings. Or you can make it by hand using the following materials:

- ❑ Card stock, sentence strip, or other heavy paper for back page (I like to use a strip the size of two index cards—approximately 10" long x 3" tall)
- ❑ 3 x 5 cards to use for the individual flip cards
- ❑ A method of binding the "book"—spiral binding or binder rings

Directions for Assembly

From the CD:

1. Print the Sentence Builder Starters. You can laminate them if you wish.

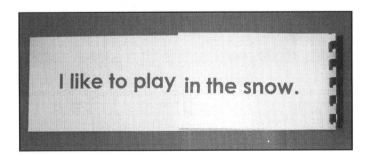

I like to play in the snow.

---

2. Print the Sentence Builder Flip Cards. There is one sheet of six completer words for each of the nine sentence starters provided. Laminate them if you wish.

3. Bind the six relevant flip cards to each of the sentence starters, on the right-hand side.

4. You can use the blank templates to create your own books or to supplement the ones provided, if you wish.

By hand with markers or using a computer:

1. Program the back "page" by writing the sentence stem on the left-hand side of the 10 x 3 strip. Try to space the stem so that it only covers half of the sentence strip to allow room for the flip cards.

2. Write individual sentence completer words on the 3 x 5 cards, and bind to the back page on the right-hand side of the book.

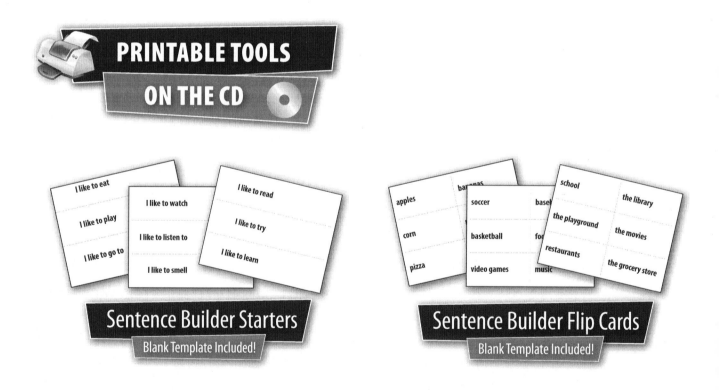

ADAPTED BOOKS
ACTIVITY

What It Is

An adapted book is a book that has been altered to serve a specific purpose or address a specific learning need. I adapt books for my students by simplifying the vocabulary and/or the sentence structure of an actual children's book (with apologies to the original author, of course!). This enables my beginning readers to read a "real" book independently and fluently.

Why It Works!

With adapted books, children feel successful reading! The complexity of the vocabulary and the sentence structure are tailored to meet the child's individual abilities and can be changed as the child's reading skills improve.

Materials Needed

- ❑ A book to adapt (board books work wonderfully because they're sturdy, but any type of book will do)
- ❑ Clear Contact™ paper or tape
- ❑ Adapted text, handwritten or printed from a word processing program or a graphics program, such as Boardmaker™

Example

Adaptation of *Little Cloud* by Eric Carle

The cloud is in the sky.

The cloud is over the house.

The cloud is big.

The cloud looks like a sheep.

The cloud looks like an airplane.

The cloud looks like a shark.

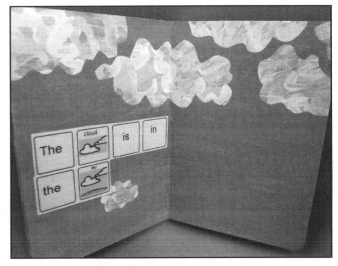

The cloud looks like a tree.

The cloud looks like a rabbit.

The cloud looks like a hat.

The cloud looks like a clown.

The cloud is all alone.

The cloud is raining.

How To Make An Adapted Book

Books can be adapted any number of ways. You'll have to experiment to find what works best for you and your students. The method described below works particularly well with board books since the pages are sturdy and the adapted text can be removed easily and replaced with new adaptations as your child's abilities increase. The original text is still intact beneath the taped-on adaptations.

1. Decide how you will alter the text, paying attention to the illustrations on each page to ensure that your adapted text aligns with the illustrations.
2. Print the adapted text, using Boardmaker™ or some other program that provides graphic support in addition to text, if needed.
3. Attach the adapted text over the original text in the book. Cover with clear Contact™ paper or clear tape.

For books with traditional paper pages, you may wish to cover the original text with Contact™ paper or tape first, before affixing your adaptation. This will preserve the original pages so you won't rip them when you remove your taped-on adaptations.

Additionally, some teachers buy two or three copies of a book to adapt. One copy remains in its original form for traditional use; one copy can be cut apart to make an adapted book (sometimes both copies are cut apart if illustrations are printed on the front and back of pages). Some teachers will cut the illustrations out and use them to make a "new" book—print the adapted text and attach the illustration that has been cut out from the original book to the adapted text page. The adapted pages can then be laminated or put in clear page protectors and bound.

Online Resources for Adapted Books

http://www.ncatp.org
Go to: Links to Resources > NCATP Staff Presentations > The American Occupational Therapy Association Conference 06 > A-Z of Adapting Books (Text Handout).
(an A-Z resource of adapting books for students with disabilities)

http://www.adaptedstories.com
(online adapted story subscription and other good stuff)

http://www.baltimorecityschools.org
Click on the Students tab. Then select Assistive Technology > Adapted Library > List All Books.
(over 500 books already adapted for you to download!)

http://www.starfall.com/n/level-a/learn-to-read/play.htm?f
(free books for reading instruction)

SOME FINAL THOUGHTS

Autism is a complex disability. Reading is a complex process. Yet even simple strategies like those presented in this book can help your child or student begin the process of reading and enjoying literature—and the world we live in!

Start small. Start simply. Explore letters and sounds. Explore words. Explore all kinds of text. Take trips to the library. Find words around you. Make up words! Write stories about your experiences. Write stories about your interests. Read them! Make time for reading. Make reading fun.

Again, I will share some encouragement from one who has instilled a love of reading in children the world over, young and old:

"You're off to Great Places!

Today is your day!

Your mountain is waiting.

So ... get on your way!"

—Dr. Seuss

From *Oh, the Places You'll Go!*

REFERENCES & RESOURCES

Cited Reading Research

Kame'enui, E. J., Simmons, D. C., Baker, S., Chard, D. J., Dickson, S. V., Gunn, B., Smith, S. B., Sprick, M., & Lin, S. J. (1997). Effective strategies for teaching beginning reading. In E. J. Kame'enui, & D. W. Carnine (Eds.), *Effective Teaching Strategies That Accommodate Diverse Learners.* Columbus, OH: Merrill.

The National Reading Panel: Teaching Children to Read—A Summary Report. (April 2000). National Institute of Child Health and Human Development.

Armbruster, B., Lehr, F., and Osborn, J. Adler, C. (ed.) (2001). *Put Reading First: The Research Building Blocks for Teaching Children to Read.*

Commercial Products

For Boardmaker™ and other wonderful products:

DynaVox Mayer-Johnson
2100 Wharton Street, Suite 400
Pittsburgh, PA 15203
Phone: 800-588-4548
Fax: 866-585-6260
Email: mayer-johnson.usa@mayer-johnson.com
Website: www.mayer-johnson.com

Fridge Phonics® can be purchased from LeapFrog Enterprises, Inc. online at www.leapfrog.com or in many local stores that sell toys. Also check out Fridge Words®, another of my favorite products for children ready to put three letters together to form words!

For tons of visual, manipulative, fun educational materials:

Lakeshore® Learning Materials
2695 E. Dominguez St.
Carson, CA 90895
Phone: 800-778-4456
Website: www.lakeshorelearning.com

For Language Master and related products:

Drake Educational Associates
St Fagans Road
Fairwater, Cardiff
United Kingdom CF5 3AE
Email: Enquiries@DrakeED.com
Website: www.Drakeed.us

For products to create your own literacy materials, including blank (bare) books, game boards, and more, check out www.barebooks.com

Treetop Publishing
PO Box 320725
Franklin, WI 53132
Phone: 800-255-9228
Fax: 888-201-5916
Website: www.barebooks.com

For Picture Me Reading!© materials:

"Picture Me Reading!"
3899 Kenwood Drive
Spring Valley, CA 91977-1024
Phone or fax: 619-462-3938 / 800-235-6822
Email: picturemereading@cox.net
Website: www.picturemereading.com

Two of my favorite visual organizer resource books are *Charts for Children* by Judy Nyberg (Good Year Books, 2007) and *Great Graphic Organizers to Use with Any Book* by Michelle O'Brien-Palmer (Scholastic, 1999).

A to Zoo: Subject Access to Children's Picture Books, Eighth Edition by Carolyn W. Lima and Rebecca L. Thomas (Libraries Unlimited, 2010). This comprehensive reference lists thousands of children's picture books, fiction and nonfiction, by subject, bibliographic information, title, and author/illustrator. You can find a book for any subject!

Online

http://www.starfall.com
(letter-sound games, free books for reading instruction, and more!)

www.inspiration.com
Inspiration™ and Kidspiration™ are computer software programs you can use to create visual organizers.

http://www.ncatp.org
Go to: Links to Resources > NCATP Staff Presentations > The American Occupational Therapy Association Conference 06 > A-Z of Adapting Books (Text Handout).
(an A-Z resource of adapting books for students with disabilities)

http://www.adaptedstories.com
(online adapted story subscription and other good stuff)

http://www.baltimorecityschools.org
Click on the Students tab. Then select Assistive Technology > Adapted Library > List All Books.
(over 500 books already adapted for you to download!)

Some other websites that might be of interest:

http://www.doe.k12.de.us/infosuites/students_family/reading/files/reading_qarsandstances.pdf

http://www.intercom.net/local/school/sdms/mspap/stances.html

http://www.readingassessment.info/resources/publications/readingandautism.htm

And, of course …

I Can Read With My Eyes Shut by Dr. Seuss (1978). Random House.

Oh, the Places You'll Go! by Dr. Seuss (1990). Random House.

INDEX

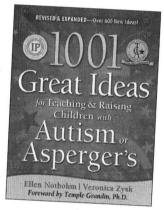

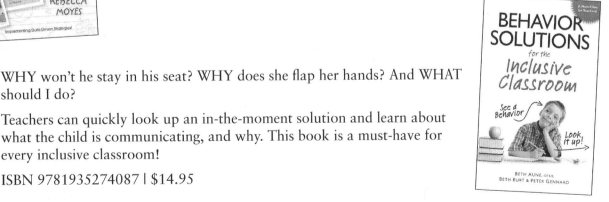